Cambridge Young Learners English Tests

Cambridge Starters 1

Answer Booklet

Examination papers from the

University of Cambridge

Local Examinations Syndicate

CAMBRIDGE
UNIVERSITY PRESS

PUBLISHED BY THE PRESS SYNDICATE OF THE UNIVERSITY OF CAMBRIDGE
The Pitt Building, Trumpington Street, Cambridge, United Kingdom

CAMBRIDGE UNIVERSITY PRESS
The Edinburgh Building, Cambridge CB2 2RU, UK
40 West 20th Street, New York, NY 10011-4211, USA
477 Williamstown Road, Port Melbourne, VIC 3207, Australia
Ruiz de Alarcón 13, 28014 Madrid, Spain
Dock House, The Waterfront, Cape Town 8001, South Africa

http:/www.cambridge.org

First published 1999
Sixth printing 2004

Printed in Italy by Legoprint S.p.A.

ISBN 0 521 65904 3 Student's Book
ISBN 0 521 66766 6 Answer Booklet
ISBN 0 521 65901 9 Cassette

Contents

Introduction   4

Practice Test 1 Answers   6

Practice Test 2 Answers   10

Practice Test 3 Answers   14

Thematic Vocabulary List 18

Introduction

The *Cambridge Young Learners English Tests* offer an elementary-level testing system for learners of English between the ages of 7 and 12. The tests include 3 key levels of assessment: *Starters*, *Movers* and *Flyers*.

Starters is the lowest level in the system and is designed for children from the age of 7 who have completed 1 year or about 100 hours of learning. However, this is very general, and there is likely to be considerable variation from country to country. Test instructions are very simple and consist only of words and structures specified in the syllabus.

The complete test lasts 45 minutes, and has the following components:
Listening, Reading/Writing and Speaking.

	length	number of parts	number of items
Listening	20 minutes	4	20
Reading and Writing	20 minutes	5	25
Speaking	5 minutes	2	–

Candidates need a pen or pencil for the Reading and Writing paper, and coloured pens or pencils for the Listening paper. All answers are written on the question papers.

Listening

In general, the aim is to focus on the 'here and now' and to use language in meaningful contexts. In addition to multiple choice and short answer questions, candidates are asked to use coloured pencils to mark their responses to some tasks. There are 4 parts. Each part begins with a clear example.

Part	skill focus	input	expected response	number of items
1	listening for lexical items and position	picture and dialogue	carrying out instructions and positioning things correctly on a picture	5
2	listening for numbers and spelling	picture and dialogue	very simple dictation; writing down numbers and spelling	5
3	listening for actions (present continuous)	pictures and dialogues	3-option multiple choice (pictures; tick the correct picture)	5
4	listening for lexis and relative position	picture and dialogue	carrying out instructions, locating, drawing and colouring correctly	5

Reading and Writing

Again, the focus is on the 'here and now' and the use of language in meaningful contexts where possible. To complete the test, candidates need a single pen or pencil of any colour. There are 5 parts, each starting with a clear example.

Part	skill focus	input	expected response	number of items
1	reading for recognition of lexis	5 lexical items with pictures	indicating 'true' with a tick or 'false' with a cross	5
2	reading for recognition of lexis, number, location and grammar	1 picture 5 sentences	writing 'yes'/'no'	5
3	spelling writing	5 pictures 5 'letter-sack's	writing words	5
4	reading writing	story-cloze with picture prompts	gap-filling (prompted); one-word answers	5
5	reading writing	story presented through 3 pictures with 5 questions	writing one-word answers to questions	5

Speaking

In the Speaking test, the candidate speaks with 1 examiner for about 5 minutes. The format of the test is explained in advance to the child in their native language, by a teacher or person familiar to them. This person then takes the child into the exam room and introduces them to the examiner.

Speaking ability is assessed according to various criteria, including comprehension, ability to produce an appropriate response, and pronunciation.

Part	input	expected response
1	greeting and name check; questions and instructions from the examiner, relating to picture prompts	carrying out verbal instructions; answering questions with appropriate actions and/or one-word responses
2	questions from the examiner on name, age, family, school class, likes, dislikes	answering questions with single words and/or short phrases

Further information

The topics, structures, words and tasks upon which the *Cambridge Young Learners English Tests* are based are comprehensively described in the handbook, so teachers or parents can know exactly what to expect.

Further information about the *Cambridge Young Learners English Tests* can be obtained from the Local Secretary for UCLES examinations in your area, or from:

EFL Division (YLE Subject Officer)
UCLES
1 Hills Road
Cambridge
CB1 2EU
United Kingdom

Telephone: +44 1223 553997
Fax: +44 1223 460278

Test 1 Answers

Listening

Part 1
There should be a line between:
1 the elephant and the boat
2 the spider and the bicycle
3 the crocodile and the car
4 the duck and the helicopter
5 the frog and the train

Part 2
1 5   2 Brown   3 3   4 Pat   5 7

Part 3
1 ✓ ☐ ☐   2 ☐ ✓ ☐   3 ✓ ☐ ☐
4 ✓ ☐ ☐   5 ☐ ☐ ✓

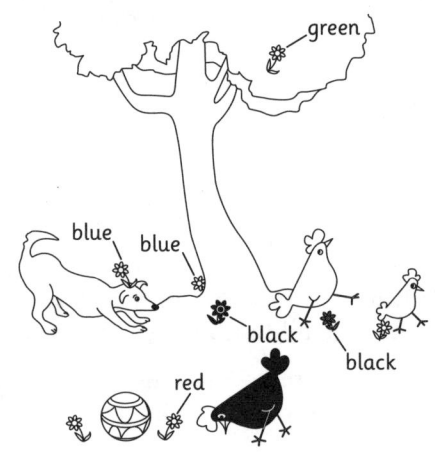

Part 4
1 The flower in the tree: green
2 The flower behind the tree: blue
3 The flower between the ball and the black hen: red
4 The flower under the big, white hen: black
5 There should be a blue flower on the dog's head

TRANSCRIPT   *Hello. This is the University of Cambridge Starters Practice Listening Test 1.*

[pause]

Look at Part 1. Now look at the picture.

[pause]

Part 1   *Listen and look. There is one example.*

Man: Put the cat in the bus.

Girl: Put what in the bus?
Man: The cat. Put the cat in the bus.

[pause}

Can you see the line? Now you listen and draw lines.

1

Man: Put the elephant in the boat.
Girl: What?
Man: The elephant. Put the elephant in the boat.

[pause]

2

Man: Put the spider on the bicycle.
Girl: Sorry? What?
Man: The spider is on the bicycle.

[pause]

3

Man: Put the crocodile in the car.
Girl: What's in the car?
Man: The crocodile. Put it in the car.

[pause]

4

Man: The duck is flying the helicopter.
Girl: Pardon?
Man: The helicopter. Put the duck in the helicopter.

[pause]

5

Man: The frog. Put the frog in the train.
Girl: Where did you say?
Man: In the train.

[pause]

Now listen to Part 1 again.

[The recording is repeated.]

[pause]

That is the end of Part 1.

[pause]

Part 2   *Look at the pictures. Listen and look.*
           There are two examples.

[pause]

Woman: Hello! What's your name?
Sam: My name is Sam.
Woman: How do you spell it?
Sam: S – A – M

[pause]

Woman: How old are you, Sam?
Sam: I'm 10 years old.
Woman: 10?
Sam: Yes. It was my birthday last week!

[pause]

Can you see the answers?
Now you listen and write a name
or a number.

1

Woman: Sam, which class are you in at school?
Sam: I'm in class five.
Woman: Five?
Sam: Yes. I like it. It's a good class to be in.

[pause]

2

Woman: What's your teacher's name?
Sam: He's called Mr Brown.
Woman: How do you spell that?
Sam: B – R – O – W – N.
Woman: B – R – O – W – N. Mr Brown.
Sam: We all like him.

[pause]

3

Woman: Do you have a good classroom?
Sam: I think so. I like it.
Woman: What number is your classroom?
Sam: It's number three. Next to the dining room.
Woman: Oh. Yes, three **is** a good room.

[pause]

4

Woman: Do you have a sister at this school?
Sam: Yes! I do.
Woman: What's her name?
Sam: Her name is Pat.
Woman: Can you spell that for me?

Sam: Of course. It's P – A – T.
Woman: P – A – T. Pat. What a pretty name!

[pause]

5

Sam: Are you an English teacher?
Woman: Yes I am.
Sam: Which class do you teach?
Woman: I teach class seven.
Sam: Class seven?
Woman: Yes.
Sam: That's my sister's class!

[pause]

Now listen to Part 2 again.

[pause]

That is the end of Part 2.

[pause]

Part 3   *Look at the pictures. Now listen and*
           look. There is one example. What's
           Bill doing?

Boy: Is Bill writing a letter?
Girl: No, he isn't. He's drawing.
Boy: Is he drawing a picture of a train?
Girl: No, he isn't. He's drawing a picture of
        a bus.

[pause]

Can you see the tick? Now you listen
and tick the box.

1 *What's Tom playing?*

Girl: Is Tom watching television?
Boy: No, he's playing in the garden.
Girl: Is he playing football?
Boy: No he isn't. He's playing basketball.

[pause]

2 *What's Nick doing?*

Girl: Do you know where Nick is? Is he
        playing football with his father?
Boy: No, he isn't. He's in the kitchen, talking.
Girl: Is he talking to his mother?
Boy: No. He's phoning a friend.

[pause]

3 *What's Ben doing?*

Girl: Is Ben playing in his bedroom?
Boy: No, he isn't. He's in bed.
Girl: Is he reading a book?
Boy: No. He's sleeping.

[pause]

4 What's Kim doing?

Boy: Is Kim playing the piano?
Girl: No, she isn't. She's playing table tennis.
Boy: Is she playing with her brother?
Girl: No. Her brother's watching television. Kim's playing table tennis with a friend.

[pause]

5 What's Ann painting?

Boy: Is Ann reading a book?
Girl: No. She's painting.
Boy: Is she painting a picture of flowers?
Girl: No. Oh no! She's painting a picture of a monster!

[pause]

Now listen to Part 3 again.

[The recording is repeated.]

[pause]

That is the end of Part 3.

[pause]

Part 4   *Look at the picture.*

[pause]

Listen and look. There is one example.

Woman: Find the flower in front of the tree.
Boy: Which flower?
Woman: The flower in front of the tree.
Boy: Yes.
Woman: Colour it black. Colour the flower in front of the tree black.

[pause]

Can you see the black flower?
Now you listen and colour.
1

Woman: Find the flower in the tree.
Boy: Where?
Woman: In the tree.
Boy: Yes.
Woman: Colour it green. Colour the flower in the tree green.

[pause]

2

Woman: Find the flower **behind** the tree.
Boy: Sorry?
Woman: The flower behind the tree.
Boy: Yes.
Woman: Colour it blue. Colour the flower behind the tree blue.

[pause]

3

Woman: Find the flower between the ball and the black hen.
Boy: What did you say?
Woman: The flower between the ball and the black hen.
Boy: OK.
Woman: Colour it red. Colour the flower between the ball and the black hen red.

[pause]

4

Woman: Find the flower under the big, white hen.
Boy: Under which white hen?
Woman: The big, white hen.
Boy: OK.
Woman: Colour it black. Colour the flower under the big, white hen black.

[pause]

5

Woman: Can you see the dog?
Boy: Yes.
Woman: Draw a flower on the dog's head.
Boy: Draw one?! On the dog's head?!
Woman: Yes! Draw a flower on the dog's head and colour it blue.
Boy: Blue!
Woman: Yes. Colour the flower on the dog's head blue!

[pause]

Now you will hear Part 4 again.

[pause]

That is the end of the Starters listening test 1.

Reading and Writing

Part 1

1 ✓   2 ✓   3 ✗   4 ✗   5 ✓

Part 2

1 yes   2 yes   3 no   4 yes   5 no

Part 3

1 mouth   2 hand   3 nose   4 feet   5 face

Part 4

1 window   2 flowers   3 books   4 desk   5 shirt

Part 5

1 ball   2 plane   3 4/four   4 swimming/playing
5 bird

Speaking

Examiner/Usher does this:	Examiner says this:	Minimum response expected from child:	Back-up questions:
Usher brings candidate in. Usher settles candidate in, using L1, then says to examiner **Hello, this is Elena**.	Hello, Elena.	Hello	
points to scene card	**Look at this. This is a living room. The children are playing. Elena, where's the boy? Where's the lamp?**	points at items in the picture	
points to object cards	**Now look at these. Which is the dog? I'm putting the dog next to the girl.**	points to object card	**Is this the dog?** (pointing to the dog)
	Now you put the dog next to the boy.	puts the object card in place (next to the boy)	**Where's the boy?**
	Which is the book?	points to object card	**Is this the book?** (pointing to the book)
	Put the book in front of the TV.	puts object card in place (in front of the TV)	**Where's the TV?**
	Which is the sock?	points to object card	**Is this the sock?** (pointing to the sock)
	Put the sock on the mat.	puts object card in place (on the mat)	**Where's the mat?**
removes object cards and points to green armchair in scene card	**Now, Elena, what's this?** **What colour is it?** **How many armchairs are there?**	**armchair** **green** **four**	**Is it an armchair?** **Is it green?** **One? Two?**
points to the boy	**What's the boy doing?**	**drawing a picture**	**Is he drawing?**
puts scene cards away and picks out 3 object cards.			
shows banana card	**What's this?** **Do you like bananas?** **What fruit do you like?**	**banana** **yes/no** **mangoes**	**Is it a banana?** **Do you like mangoes?**
shows pen/clock card	**What's this?** **What colour is it?** **Have you got a pen/clock?**	**pen/clock** **blue/red** **yes/no**	**Is it a pen/clock?** **Is it blue/red?**
shows mouse card	**What's this?** **Do you like mice?** **What animals do you like?**	**mouse** **yes/no** **cats**	**Is it a mouse?** **Do you like cats?**
puts away all cards	**Now, Elena, how old are you?** **What's your favourite sport?** **What's your friend's name?**	**7** **tennis** **Mary**	**Are you 7? 8?** **Do you like tennis?** **Is your friend's name Mary?**
	OK, thank you, Elena. Good-bye.	**Good-bye.**	

Test 2 Answers

Listening

Part 1

There should be a line between:

1 the banana and a place in front of the window
2 the pineapple and a place next to the clock
3 the water melon and the box
4 the lemon and a place between the radio and the book
5 the coconut and the chair

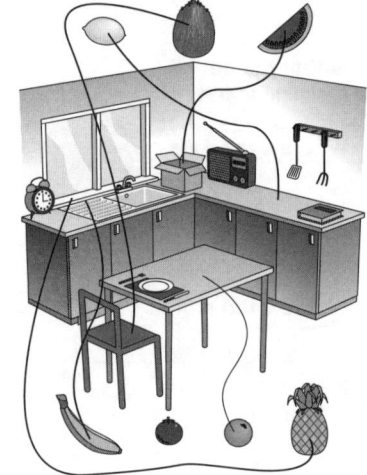

Part 2

1 Pat   2 meat   3 4/four   4 Old (Street)
5 Mary

Part 3

1 ☐ ☐ ☑   2 ☐ ☑ ☐   3 ☐ ☐ ☑
4 ☐ ☐ ☑   5 ☐ ☐ ☑

Part 4

1 fish in the bag: red
2 fish behind the boat: green
3 fish in front of the frog: yellow
4 fish between the bag and the baby: brown
5 There should be a fish next to the crocodile.

Hello. This is the University of Cambridge Starters Practice Listening Test 2.

[pause]

Part 1 Look at Part 1. Now look at the picture. Listen and look. There is one example.

[pause]

Man: The orange is on the table.
Girl: Pardon? Where?
Man: On the table, the orange is on the table.

[pause]

Can you see the line? Now you listen and draw lines.

1
Man: The banana is in front of the window.
Girl: Sorry?
Man: The banana is in front of the window.

[pause]

2
Man: The pineapple is next to the clock.
Girl: Where?
Man: The pineapple is next to the clock.

[pause]

3
Man: The water melon is in the box.
Girl: Pardon? What's in the box?
Man: The water melon.

[pause]

4
Man: The lemon is between the radio and the book.
Girl: Where?
Man: Between the radio and the book.

[pause]

5
Man: The coconut is on the chair.
Girl: Where's the coconut?
Man: On the chair.

[pause]

Now listen to Part 1 again.

[The recording is repeated.]

That is the end of Part 1.

Part 2   *Look at the pictures.*

[pause]

Listen and look. There are two examples.

Woman:	Hello. Is this your cat?
Boy:	Yes, it is.
Woman:	What's his name?
Boy:	Nick.
Woman:	How do you spell that?
Boy:	N – I – C – K.

[pause]

Woman:	How old's Nick?
Boy:	He's three.
Woman:	Three?
Boy:	Yes. Nick's very young.

[pause]

Can you see the answers?
Now you listen and write a name or a number.

1

Woman:	Is this your dog?
Boy:	Yes, it is.
Woman:	What's her name?
Boy:	Her name's Pat.
Woman:	Pat? How do you spell that?
Boy:	P – A – T.
Woman:	Pat. That's a nice name.

[pause]

2

Woman:	What's Pat's favourite food?
Boy:	She likes meat.
Woman:	Oh!
Boy:	Yes, she loves it.

[pause]

3

Woman:	Is this your house?
Boy:	Yes, it is.
Woman:	How many bedrooms has it got?
Boy:	It's got four.
Woman:	It's a big house.

[pause]

4

Woman:	Where is this?
Boy:	It's my street.
Woman:	What's the name of your street?
Boy:	Old Street.
Woman:	Old Street, how do you spell that?
Boy:	O – L – D, Old Street.

[pause]

5

Woman:	Is this your sister?
Boy:	No, she's my friend.
Woman:	What's her name?
Boy:	Her name's Mary.
Woman:	How do you spell that?
Boy:	M – A – R – Y.
Woman:	That's a very nice name.

[pause]

Now listen to Part 2 again.

[The recording is repeated.]

That is the end of Part 2.

Part 3   *Look at the pictures.*

[pause]

Now listen and look. There is one example. What's Sue playing with?

Girl:	Where's Sue?
Boy:	She's in the garden.
Girl:	Is she playing football?
Boy:	No, she's playing with her new kite.

[pause]

Can you see the tick? Now you listen and tick the box.

1 *What's Tom doing?*

[pause]

Girl:	Where's Tom? Is he playing football?
Boy:	No, he's in the living room, taking a photo.
Girl:	He isn't playing his new guitar?
Boy:	No, he doesn't like it.

[pause]

2 *Where's Mummy?*

[pause]

Boy:	Where's Mummy now?
Girl:	She's in the house.
Boy:	Is she writing at her desk?
Girl:	No, she's talking to a friend in the dining room.

[pause]

3 *What's Daddy doing?*

[pause]

Boy:	Is Daddy in the garden?
Girl:	No, he's in the living room playing the piano.

Boy: Oh, he listens to the radio or watches TV in the afternoon.
Girl: Not today.

[pause]

4 What game are Sam and Pat playing?

[pause]

Girl: I can't find Sam and Pat.
Boy: They're playing in Sam's bedroom.
Girl: Are they playing table tennis?
Boy: No, they're playing a game on Sam's computer.

[pause]

5 What's Grandfather doing?
[pause]

Boy: Is Grandfather sleeping in the house?
Girl: No, he's in the garden.
Boy: He doesn't sleep in the garden!
Girl: No, he's reading a book.

[pause]

Now listen to Part 3 again.

[The recording is repeated.]

That is the end of Part 3.

Part 4   *Look at the picture.*

[pause]

Listen and look. There is one example.

Woman: Find the fish in the sea.
Boy: Sorry?
Woman: The fish in the sea.
Boy: Yes.
Woman: Colour it blue. Colour the fish blue.

[pause]

Can you see the blue fish? Now you listen and colour.

1

Woman: Find the fish in the bag.
Boy: Sorry?
Woman: Find the fish in the bag.
Boy: OK.
Woman: Colour it red. Colour the fish red.

[pause]

2
Woman: Can you see the fish behind the boat?
Boy: Where?
Woman: Behind the boat.
Boy: Yes.
Woman: Colour the fish green.
Boy: OK. Green.

[pause]

3
Woman: Find the fish in front of the frog.
Boy: Sorry, where's the fish?
Woman: In front of the frog.
Boy: Oh yes.
Woman: Colour it yellow. Colour this fish yellow.

[pause]

4
Woman: Can you see the fish between the bag and the baby?
Boy: Pardon? Which fish?
Woman: Between the bag and the baby.
Boy: Oh yes.
Woman: Colour it brown. Colour this fish brown.

[pause]

5
Woman: Can you see the crocodile?
Boy: Yes.
Woman: Draw a fish on the beach next to it.
Boy: Sorry?
Woman: Draw a fish next to the crocodile.

[pause]

Now you will hear Part 4 again.

[The recording is repeated.]

That is the end of the Starters listening test 2.

Reading and Writing

Part 1

| 1 ✓ | 2 ✓ | 3 ✗ | 4 ✓ | 5 ✗ |

Part 2

| 1 yes | 2 no | 3 yes | 4 yes | 5 no |

Part 3

1 tennis   2 hockey   3 baseball   4 fishing   5 kite

Part 4

1 bedroom   2 black   3 football   4 monsters
5 TV

Part 5

1 brown   2 2/two   3 sitting   4 tree   5 cake

Speaking

Examiner/Usher does this:	Examiner says this:	Minimum response expected from child:	Back-up questions:
Usher brings candidate in. Usher settles candidate in, using L1, then says to examiner, **Hello, this is Fabrice.**	**Hello Fabrice.**	**Hello**	
points to scene card	**Look at this. It's a beautiful day. The family are having lunch. Fabrice, where's the boy? Where's the duck?**	points at items in the picture	
points to object cards	**Now look at these. Which is the bag? I'm putting the bag next to the girl.**	points to object card	**Is this the bag?** (pointing to the bag)
	Now you put the bag under the tree.	puts object card in place (under the tree)	**Where's the tree?**
	Which is the radio?	points to object card	**Is this the radio?** (pointing to the radio)
	Put the radio next to the boy.	puts object card in place (next to the boy)	**Where's the boy?**
	Which is the boat?	points to object card	**Is this the boat?** (pointing to the boat)
	Put the boat in the water.	puts object card in place (in the water)	**Where's the water?**
removes object cards and points to red ball in scene card	**Now, Fabrice, what's this? What colour is it? How many balls are there?**	**ball** **red** **three**	**Is it a ball? Is it red?** **One? Two?**
points to the father	**What's the father doing?**	**kicking a ball**	**Is he kicking?**
puts scene cards away and picks out 3 object cards			
shows frog card	**What's this? Have you got a frog? What animals do you like?**	**frog** **yes/no** **dogs**	**Is it a frog?** **Do you like dogs?**
shows jacket/dress card	**What's this? What colour is it? What's your favourite colour?**	**jacket/dress** **blue/pink** **green**	**Is it a jacket/dress? Is it blue/pink?** **Is it green?**
shows pineapple/fish card	**What's this? Do you like pineapples/fish? What do you eat for lunch?**	**pineapple/fish** **yes/no** **burgers**	**Is it a pineapple?** **Do you like burgers?**
puts away all cards	**Now, Fabrice, where do you live?**	**Paris**	**Do you live in Paris?**
	How many brothers and sisters have you got? What's your father's name?	**3 brothers** **Jean**	**Have you got a brother? Is your father's name Jean?**
	OK, thank you, Fabrice. Good-bye.	**Good-bye.**	

13

Test 3 Answers

Listening

Part 1

There should be a line between:

1 the T-shirt and the cupboard
2 the clock and the wall, between the two pictures
3 the shoe and under the bath
4 the radio and the mirror
5 the snake and a place next to the crocodile

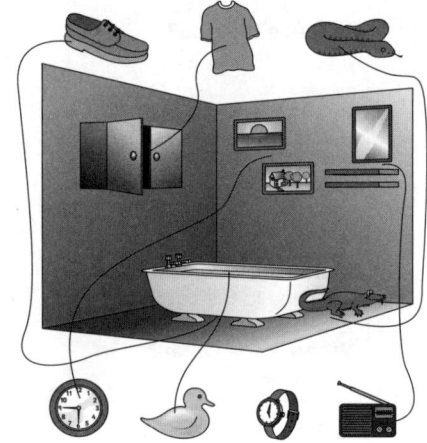

Part 2

1 Sam   2 9   3 3   4 Sue   5 Story (Street)

Part 3

1 ☐ ☐ ✓   2 ✓ ☐ ☐   3 ✓ ☐ ☐
4 ☐ ✓ ☐   5 ☐ ✓ ☐

Part 4

1 the ball in the box: blue
2 the ball under the tree: red
3 the ball behind the bag: green
4 the ball next to the flowers: pink
5 There should be a purple ball next to the dog.

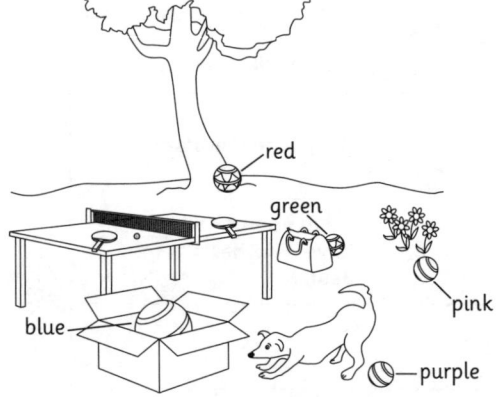

Hello. This is the University of Cambridge Starters Practice Listening Test 3.

[pause]

Part 1 *Look at Part 1. Now look at the picture. Listen and look. There is one example.*

Man: The duck is in the bath.
Girl: Pardon? Where?
Man: The duck is in the bath.

[pause]

Can you see the line? Now you listen and draw lines.

1

Man: The T-shirt is in the cupboard.
Girl: Sorry. Where?
Man: The T-shirt is in the cupboard.

[pause]

2

Man: The clock is on the wall.
Girl: Where's the clock?
Man: On the wall, between the two pictures.

[pause]

3

Man: The shoe is under the bath.
Girl: Pardon?
Man: The shoe is under the bath.

[pause]

4

Man: The radio is in front of the mirror.
Girl: Sorry? Where's the radio?
Man: In front of the mirror.

[pause]

5

Man: The snake is next to the crocodile.
Girl: What's next to the crocodile?
Man: The snake.

[pause]

Now listen to Part 1 again.

[The recording is repeated.]

That is the end of Part 1.

Part 2   *Look at the pictures.*

[pause]

Listen and look. There are two
examples.

Man:	Hello. What's your name?
Girl:	May.
Man:	How do you spell that?
Girl:	M – A – Y.
Man:	That's a nice name.

[pause]

Man:	How old are you, May?
Girl:	I'm eight.
Man:	Eight?
Girl:	Yes.

[pause]

Can you see the answers?
Now you listen and write a name
or a number.

1

Man:	Is this your brother?
Girl:	Yes, it is.
Man:	What's his name?
Girl:	His name's Sam.
Man:	How do you spell that?
Girl:	S – A– M.
Man:	That's a nice name.

[pause]

2

Man:	And how old is Sam?
Girl:	He's nine.
Man:	Nine?
Girl:	Yes, it's his birthday today.

[pause]

3

Man:	Is this your school?
Girl:	Yes, it is.
Man:	How many teachers have you got?
Girl:	I've got three.
Man:	Three! That's nice.

[pause]

4

Man:	Who's this?
Girl:	My Grandmother.
Man:	What's her name?
Girl:	Sue.
Man:	How do you spell that?
Girl:	S – U – E.

[pause]

5

Man:	And where does she live?
Girl:	She lives in Story Street.
Man:	Sorry?
Girl:	Story Street.
Man:	Right.

[pause]

Now listen to Part 2 again.

[The recording is repeated.]

That is the end of Part 2.

Part 3   *Look at the pictures.*

[pause]

Now listen and look. There is
one example. What's Tom doing?

Girl:	Where's Tom?
Boy:	He's playing with a ball in the garden.
Girl:	What's he doing?
Boy:	He's kicking it.

[pause]

Can you see the tick? Now you
listen and tick the box.

1 What's Sue doing?

[pause]

Girl:	Where's Sue?
Boy:	She's in the classroom.
Girl:	Is she reading?
Boy:	No, she's sleeping on her desk.

[pause]

2 Where are the children?

[pause]

Boy:	Where are the children now?
Girl:	They're at school.
Boy:	Oh, they're learning English today.
Girl:	No they're not, they're singing.

[pause]

3 What's the teacher doing?

Boy:	Is the teacher here today?
Girl:	Yes, he's in the classroom.
Boy:	What's he doing?
Girl:	He's writing letters on the board.

[pause]

4 What are the girls eating?

[pause]

Girl: I can't find Sue and Mary.
Boy: They're having lunch in the kitchen.
Girl: Are they eating cake?
Boy: No, they're eating bananas.

[pause]

5 What game are the boys playing?

[pause]

Boy: Are the boys in the garden?
Girl: No, they're playing in the living room with their toys.
Boy: What game are they playing?
Girl: They're playing with robots.

[pause]

Now listen to Part 3 again.

[The recording is repeated.]

That is the end of Part 3.

Part 4 *Look at the picture.*

[pause]

Listen and look. There is one example.

Woman: Find the ball on the table.
Boy: Sorry?
Woman: The ball on the table.
Boy: Yes.
Woman: Colour it yellow. Colour this ball yellow.

[pause]

Can you see the yellow ball?
Now you listen and colour.

1

Woman: Find the ball in the box.
Boy: Sorry?
Woman: Find the ball in the box.
Boy: OK.
Woman: Colour it blue. Colour it blue.

[pause]

2

Woman: Can you see the ball under the tree?
Boy: Where?
Woman: Under the tree.
Boy: Yes.
Woman: Colour this ball red.

[pause]

3

Woman: Find the ball behind the bag.
Boy: Sorry?
Woman: Find the ball behind the bag.
Boy: Oh yes.
Woman: Colour it green.
Boy: Green?
Woman: Yes.

[pause]

4

Woman: Can you see the ball next to the flowers?
Boy: Pardon?
Woman: The ball next to the flowers.
Boy: Oh yes.
Woman: Colour it pink. Colour this ball pink.

[pause]

5

Woman: Can you see the dog?
Boy: Yes.
Woman: Draw a ball next to the dog.
Boy: Sorry?
Woman: Draw a ball next to the dog and then colour it purple.

[pause]

Now you will hear Part 4 again.

[The recording is repeated.]

That is the end of the Starters listening test 3.

Reading and Writing

Part 1

1 ✗   2 ✓   3 ✓   4 ✗   5 ✓

Part 2

1 no   2 yes   3 yes   4 no   5 yes

Part 3

1 carrot   2 potato   3 chicken   4 tomato   5 meat

Part 4

1 jacket   2 (hand)bag   3 trees   4 blue   5 pencil

Part 5

1 flying   2 4/four   3 ball   4 pointing/laughing
5 ice cream

Examiner/Usher does this:	Examiner says this:	Minimum response expected from child:	Back-up questions:
Usher brings candidate in. Usher settles candidate in, using L1, then says to examiner, **Hello, this is Anna.**	**Hello, Anna.**	**Hello**	
points to scene card	**Look at this. This is the beach. The family are having a day at the sea. Anna, where's the boy? Where's the hat?**	points at items in the picture	
points to object cards	**Now look at these. Which is the radio? I'm putting the radio next to the girl.**	points to object card	**Is this the radio?** (pointing to the radio)
	Now you put the radio next to the book.	puts object card in place (next to the book)	**Where's the book?**
	Which is the monster?	points to object card	**Is this the monster?** (pointing to the monster)
	Put the monster in the sea.	puts object card in place (in to the sea)	**Where's the sea?**
	Which is the ball/fish?	points to object card	**Is this the ball/fish?** (pointing to the ball/fish)
	Put the ball/fish behind the mother.	puts object card in place (behind the mother)	**Where's the mother?**
removes object cards and points to dog in scene card	**Now, Anna, what's this?** **What colour is it?** **How many dogs are there?**	**dog** **brown** **two**	**Is it a dog?** **Is it brown?** **One? Two?**
points to the mother	**What's the mother doing?**	**eating a banana**	**Is he eating?**
puts scene cards away and picks out 3 object cards			
shows camera card	**What's this?** **What colour is it?** **Have you got a camera?**	**camera** **black** **yes/no**	**Is it a camera?** **black**
shows burger/ice cream card	**What's this?**	**burger/ice cream**	**Is it a burger/an ice cream?**
	Do you like burgers/ice cream? What's your favourite food?	**yes/no** **cake**	**Is it cake?**
shows hippo card	**What's this?** **What animals do you like?**	**hippo** **dogs**	**Is it a hippo?** **Do you like dogs?**
	Have you got an animal at home?	**yes/no**	**Have you got a cat?**
puts away all cards	**Now, Anna, how old are you?** **How many brothers and sisters have you got?** **What's your mother's name?**	**7** **2 sisters** **Maria**	**Are you 7? 8?** **Have you got a sister?** **Is your mother's name Maria?**
	OK, thank you, Anna. Good-bye.	**Good-bye**	

STARTERS THEMATIC VOCABULARY LIST

For ease of reference vocabulary is arranged in semantic groups or themes.
Some words appear under more than one heading.
In addition to the topics, notions and concepts listed for the syllabus,
the following categories appear:

- miscellaneous objects/nouns
- adjectives
- functions
- verbs

ANIMALS

animal
bird
cat
chicken
cow
crocodile
dog
duck
elephant
fish (s + pl)
frog
giraffe
goat
hippo
horse
lizard
monkey
mouse/mice
sheep (s + pl)
snake
spider
tiger

THE BODY AND FACE

arm
body
ear
eye
face
foot/feet
hair
hand
head
leg
mouth
nose

CLOTHES

clothes
dress
glasses
handbag
hat
jacket
jeans
shirt
shoe
skirt
sock
trousers
T-shirt
wear

FAMILY, FRIENDS AND OURSELVES

Ann
baby
Ben
Bill
birthday
boy brother
child/children
dad(dy)
family
father
friend
girl
grandfather
grandmother
happy (birthday)
he
her
him
his

I
Kim
live
man/men
may
me
mother
mum(my)
my
name
Nic
old
Pat
Sam
she
sister
Sue
their
them
they
Tom
us
we
woman/women
you
young
your

FOOD (AND DRINK)

apple
banana
bean
bread
breakfast
burger
cake
carrot
chicken

coconut
drink (n & v)
eat
egg
fish
food
French fries
ice cream
juice
lemon
lemonade
lime
lunch
mango
meat
milk
orange
pea
pineapple
potato
rice
sausage
supper
tomato
water
watermelon

THE HOME

armchair
bath
bathroom
bed
bedroom
bookcase
box
camera
chair
clock
cupboard
dining room
doll
door
flower
garden
hall
house
kitchen
lamp
living room
mat
mirror
phone
radio
room

sleep
sofa
table
television/TV
toy
tree
watch
window

SCHOOL AND THE CLASSROOM, AND LANGUAGE AND TESTS

alphabet
answer
ask
board
book
bookcase
class
classroom
close
colour
colour (in)
correct
cross
desk
draw
English
eraser
example
find
floor
know (don't know)
learn
lesson
letter
line
listen (to)
look
no
number
open
page
part
pen
pencil
picture
question
read
right
ruler
school
sentence

teacher
tell
test
tick
understand
wall
word
write
yes

SPORTS AND LEISURE-TIME ACTIVITIES

badminton
ball
baseball
basketball
beach
book
bounce
camera
doll
draw(ing)
enjoy
favourite
fish(ing)
game
guitar
hit
hobby
hockey
kick
kite
listen (to)
paint(ing)
photo
piano
picture
play (with)
radio
read
run
sing
soccer
song
story
swim
table tennis
television/TV
tennis
toy
watch

19

TRANSPORT

bike
boat
bus
car
fly
go
helicopter
motorbike
plane
ride
run
swim
train
walk

COLOURS

black
blue
brown
green
grey (or gray)
pink
purple
red
white
yellow

LOCATION AND POSITION

at
behind
between
here
in
in front of
next to
on
there
under

ADJECTIVES

beautiful
big
clean
dirty
favourite
good
happy
new
old
right
sad
small
ugly
young

FORMULAIC EXPRESSIONS

bye (-bye)
good-bye
hello
I don't know
no
oh
OK
pardon
please
right
so
sorry
thank you
then
well
yes

MISCELLANEOUS OBJECTS/NOUNS

bag
box
computer
day
monster
night
robot
sea
street
sun

VERBS

Irregular:
be
can/cannot/can't
catch
do/don't
draw
drink
eat
find
fly
give
go
have (got)
know
learn
put
read
ride
run
say
sing
sit (down)
sleep
spell
stand (up)
swim
throw
understand
wear
write

VERBS

Regular:
answer
ask
close
colour
cross
enjoy
jump
kick
learn
like
listen (to)
live
look
love
open
paint
phone
pick up
play (with)
point
show
start
stop
talk
tick
try
walk
want
watch

DETERMINERS

a/an
no
that
the
this
these
those

ADVERBS

again
here
now
there
today
very

PREPOSITIONS

at
behind
between
in
in front of
like
next to
of
on
to
under